salmonpoetry

An Ink Like Early Twilight

ANDREA POTOS

salmonpoetry

Published in 2015 by
Salmon Poetry
Cliffs of Moher, County Clare, Ireland
Website: www.salmonpoetry.com
Email: info@salmonpoetry.com

ISBN 978-1-910669-12-9

COVER PHOTOGRAPHY: *Ollietaylorphotography | Dreamstime.com -*
Exe Estuary Twilight Night Photo
COVER DESIGN & TYPESETTING: *Siobhán Hutson*
Printed in Ireland by Sprint Print

For my irrepressible father

Acknowledgments

Grateful acknowledgement is made to the journals and magazines where many of these poems first appeared, sometimes in slightly different versions: *Adanna Journal, Atlanta Review, Cider Creek Review, Cutthroat, Earth's Daughters, Escape Into Life, Express Milwaukee, Illuminations, Literary Mama, Loch Raven Review, Naugatuck River Review, Nimrod International Journal, Off the Coast, Poetry East, Poetry Salzburg Review, poemmemoirstory, Sou'wester, Rosebud, Serving House Journal, Tiferet, Wind Magazine, Verse-Virtual, Verse Wisconsin, Voices of Hellenism.*

Several of these poems appeared in my chapbook *New Girl* (Anchor & Plume Press, 2014).

Contents

Back from Rome 11

Cafe Transport 12

When Asked Why Do I Always Leave the Country
When I Travel 13

Old Village Walk 14

Closed for Renovations 15

In the Garden of Keats 16

Johns Keats and John Constable 17

Summer Moment 18

A Boy in Greece 19

Living by Water 20

Praise Your Life 21

The Doe That Appeared on the University Athletic
Fields 22

Daughter Heart 23

Greek Easter Photograph 24

Some Questions from the Audience 25

When My Daughter Reads Aloud 26

Eternity Happened 27

Walking in Greece 28

Sun Lover 29

Clear 30

With the Elgin Marbles, Thinking of Keats 31

On Hampstead Heath 32

Infidelity in the Famous Writer's Poem 33

The Story that Narrates Worry 34

Learning Castenet 35

It Happens in Italy 36

On Viewing Caravaggio's *The Conversion of St. Paul* 37

Upon Entering Keats' House   38
John Keats, On Meeting Leigh Hunt   39
Piazza San Marco   40
Ex   41
Book Well   42
On September 19   43
At Fourteen   44
The Room Where Keats is Not   45
When the Doctor Looked at the Ultrasound of
    My Shoulder. . .   46
When the Flood   47
Early September, My Father   48
A Long Deep Run   49
Coma   50
When People Ask: How Can You Write in a Busy
    Cafe   51
Teenage Daughter   52
The Day It Happened   53
My Father, Recovering from Brain Injury   54
Following My Father   55
A Good Morning   56
Pilgrim   57
At Keats' Grave   58
Caravaggio's *Madonna of the Pilgrims*   59
Sleep After Travel   60
How to Find Keats   61

There is an awful warmth about my heart like a load of Immortality.

JOHN KEATS
in a letter to J.H. Reynolds,
September 1818

BACK FROM ROME

When people say: *Welcome back*
to the real world,
I want to tell them how I awakened
to Romans passing through the piazza
outside our windows, how one day a woman
in a red coat eating a pastry stopped to clean
her sticky fingers in the fountain that sang
even through the nights,
that men strolled with their newspapers
and cigarettes, and children chased pigeons
on the uneven cobblestones everywhere
that made me aware how it is
I walk on the face of this earth,
on my way to the *forno* where a tall,
silver-haired man sliced long slabs of
pizza bianca just emerged from the ovens,
how he smiled *Prego!* when handing me
the gold bread glistening with oil and a sprinkling
of peccorino romano, and I left to devour it
while walking in the Campo di Fiori where
vendors sold me plums and berries,
miniature bottles of limoncello and bags
of rigatoni, spaghetti, and candied almonds
that dissolved on the tongue; along with pendants
of murano glass and jackets stitched with "Italia"
in red and gold letters—Italia—that country where I
slept and breathed and dwelled for
nine spacious days, there in the Mediterranean—
on the map nearest to Albania, Croatia,
Greece, beside the life-sustaining seas.

CAFE TRANSPORT

Staring through the smudged, late-
winter window, at the wrought iron grate
and sun on brick, gold as Renaissance light,
it strikes me how it is also
March in Rome, on some piazza
where a scratched wooden table
wobbles just slightly while I sip
a cafe and listen
to cobblestones collect passing
stories of stilettos, boots and sneakers,
with Bernini's fountain in the center,
molded like a grand bathtub for pigeons
and happy drunks at 4 a.m.,
still blurbling with clear, clean music.

WHEN ASKED WHY DO I ALWAYS
LEAVE THE COUNTRY WHEN I TRAVEL

Have you ever been a bride
or a groom, betrothed
to possibility—
have you ever married the face of adventure
that looks nothing like your own?

Would you ever
like to glide through passageways
and aisles of night,
tossing the hours behind you like confetti
or blossoms,
while below you
the sea sprawls—a voluminous train rippling
with fathoms and light?

OLD VILLAGE WALK

Our guide apologized for the mist,
the modern version of London fog
obscuring the postcard sight
of the city from where we stood.
I wanted to say: forget the view
of St. Paul's from four miles off,
a glimpse of the rotating Eye.
Let me follow these twisting
stone lanes, stand on Lower Terrace
where Constable began
his first paintings of clouds and skies.
I'll walk near Millfield Lane, where Keats
encountered Coleridge just that once,
where the heath grass feels thick and luscious
under my feet. I'll gladly take the deep
green slope down to the Vale where
Leigh Hunt's cottage once stood.
Hazlitt, Byron and large Liberal thinkers
flocked there and, on that pond, Shelley,
the great Shelley, sailed his paper boats.

CLOSED FOR RENOVATIONS

Keats House, Hampstead

I loitered by the gate
until a man from the Heath Library
came up and mentioned the gap
in the wrought iron fence:
But you didn't hear that from me, he winked.
I slipped through
in a misty drizzle

to the other side
where Keats sat enthroned
in a May evening, among the grass,
the thicket and the fruit-tree wild.
All week the nightingale
called him to come out with his pen,
his loose scraps of paper.
Darkling I listen he told it, beside
the plum tree long replaced

by another, the mulberry
still melodious with green, winding *past*
the near meadows, over
the still-stream, his absence
around me as clear
as presence, a notion
he would have nodded to.

IN THE GARDEN OF KEATS

I lay down in clover grass,
my fingers dyed crimson
from the mulberries
I'd plucked off the low winding
branches that sprawled nearly to the poet's door.
Even the ivory pages of my book
were stained and smeared with a red
I would never forget,
before the docent emerged from the house
to tell me *no*,
I must not pick,
I must not eat
the fruit off the ancient,
perfect tree.

JOHN KEATS AND JOHN CONSTABLE

Hampstead, 1819.

I wonder if they ever passed one another
on Well Walk, where Keats
once nursed his brother Tom,
where Constable lived with his beloved Maria,

if they ever nodded to one another
on the Heath, with its grand view
of St. Paul's dome, its vistas of skyscapes,
stubble fields and rosy autumn hues—

the barred clouds Keats knew
would bloom his dying days,
what Constable would prove
with billowing sky studies

and ever-transforming light—
conjurer with brush,
kindred stranger with pen.

SUMMER MOMENT

A gibbous moon landed
on the crowns of the locusts.

Shrubs and trees quivered with song.
Thoughts, those sweaty

old dogs,
laid down.

Twilight, murmurous and warm,
swept into the space it was meant for.

A BOY IN GREECE

for Papouli

My grandfather was a boy
in the mountains not far
from Delphi, great navel
of Mother Earth.
He lived in a village encircled
by a silvery-green sea
of olive trees and dust,
and lit by a billion stars.
He told me he could read by
their light alone.
I love to think of him
under that luminous sky,
eons before
I was born to his gentleness.
Even the darkness
cradled him,
a book creased open on his lap.

LIVING BY WATER

Give me the nearness of water—
boats cleaving wind-brushed
gem-green, molten grey and sails
birthing full colors to air—

the way a child might wish
for the sight of her mother
through an open door,
arc of her mother¹s hands
turning the pages of her book,
stirring the broth on the stove;
the ruffling of her skirts
as she moves, her hair
accepting whatever light
passes through the window.

PRAISE YOUR LIFE

When on a June morning heavy with rain,
you can taste the best cappucino
since Rome, in a cafe
with scarred maplewood tables,
a book of Caravaggio splayed open:
The Calling of St. Mathew
that could be set in a tavern,
a gambling den, a dank office where
tax collectors are counting their day¹s work,
while in the top right of the frame, a gold-
seared light slices in, and with it,
the figure of a god made man—
a bolt of radiance shoots through
his finger, pointed as if to say: You,
it is you, I have called to this life.

THE DOE THAT APPEARED ON
THE UNIVERSITY ATHLETIC FIELDS

she leapt
into view   rose
five feet or higher   turning

in the thick summer air

she called the echoes from the grass

stopped the athletes in their games—

she pushed me off my treadmill mind

I was down on the grass
collecting awe in her wake

DAUGHTER HEART

It raps on the gates
of mine, a rust-
pocked hinge
opening
onto the place where
she waits
in salt-stained air,
out where the sun
excludes nothing,
not the sprawled blue jellyfish,
the ripped lacery of kelp,
not the beached-up bone
of some creature long gone,
scrubbed to a sheen by the sea.

GREEK EASTER PHOTOGRAPH

Last of the lamb on my grandmother's platter,
the sweet-bread loaves torn,
the body made sated.

My grandparents' hands meet
in the center of the frame,
each cups an egg,
pomegranate-red and glistening
through all the years
as if each one was polished
by Apollo.

Between them, a smile
as they pause
to rap egg
upon egg, gentle
echo of luck
that followed me into my life.

SOME QUESTIONS FROM THE AUDIENCE

Why so many cats?
Are those bars on the side of the Parthenon?
Did Socrates really
swallow the hemlock in that cave?

How many pillars make a temple?
Why an owl on top?
What did those urns hold?

Is the water always see-through?
How do the village houses, the steps
stay so white?

What do those stones mean? Tell me
how blue becomes that blue.

WHEN MY DAUGHTER READS ALOUD

I remember how she once
stumbled over *cat*,
go, the twisting
pathways
of *fox in socks*.

How did she
arrive here, this morning
before the second grade bell,
announcing *clover*, *chlorophyll*, flying
with the Magic School bus
into the heart of the chloroplast—
        she is there
when the green world wakes.

ETERNITY HAPPENED

Oia, Thira

once when the Greek sun
had its say
over the terraces and cliffs,
the lapis water of the caldera
waving and blinking *Yes.*
Even the feral tabby settled
on the veranda
where we stared,
where we breathed
stricken by beauty,
future—a word
we would not understand.

WALKING IN GREECE

Sifnos

I'm surrounded by blue
shining that nearly blinds.

Whitewashed stones wind
a path through the village—

old men at their tables,
a pack donkey tied to a tree.

Something in me
feels even

with the earth,
the weight of sun

that knows its strength.
I climb the steep path,

my grandmother's grandmother's hands
softly pressed on my back.

SUN LOVER

Face upturned, arms and legs
splayed out in tall grass,
I could be a plant taking light,
making it food,

warmth seeping through skin,
flesh on the verge
of some joyful, chemical
transformation.

I think of the faithful
who open their mouths for the wafer
dissolving, converting
to something like god in their bodies.

CLEAR

Dartmoor, England

Standing in the gorge,
surrounded by green gauze
of spring woods,
I thought of Keats, when he wrote
of his love:
I want a word that's brighter
than bright.
I watched the stream
that had its source from someplace
far.   I wanted a word
that was clearer than clear,
stiller than still
to capture that water,
a word that would sink
at once
to the depths
of what I
could not reach.

WITH THE ELGIN MARBLES,
THINKING OF KEATS

British Museum, London

I can't help thinking of you here, dazed
like unwilling sleep,
struck-still
by the onslaught of time
trapped in stone. Dionysus
reclining on the skin of a feline;
the centaur carrying off a struggling girl
who will not get away.
So do these wonders a most dizzy pain,
you wrote. You watched, as I do, the horse
of the moon goddess Selene,
weary from its nightly labor,
its bulging eyes and mouth agape.
Even contented Hestia, hearth-bound,
is like your urn, another foster child
of silence and slow time—
there she is, held, forever,
on the point of rising.

ON HAMPSTEAD HEATH
following Keats and Coleridge

I climb up Kite Hill, wind
down past the ponds. I search out
the lane near Highgate villlage where
they encountered one another
that spring Sunday in 1819 when
a high wind was filling the trees.
A young man of very striking countenance,
and Coleridge, whose voice Keats heard
upon arriving and leaving and inbetween,
that sole meeting of the two, carrying
their great caches of loss. I listen
to hear the thousands of things
they spoke of as they walked
for miles: nightingales and species
of dreams, the contrasts between will
and volition, ghosts and nightmares
and the fleetingness of poetical sensations
that might even be this birdcall—warbler
and kestrel—this swishing of grass heath,
bluebell under my feet.

INFIDELITY IN THE CONTEMPORARY FAMOUS WRITER'S POEM

Reading it, you can almost believe
in the beauty underlying
everything, the lover
waiting under the window
in the scorching air,
a lapis blue Agean
glinting in the distance,
gulls etching the sky.
No sign anywhere
of half-masts submerged,
no glimpse of Odysseus
strapped to the mast,
so very far from home.

THE STORY THAT NARRATES WORRY

was handed down,
mouth-to-mouth
from the Old Country,
kerchiefed grandmothers
wrapped in their black garb,
reciting creeds
of disaster and loss
while caring for
husbands and children,
molding the doughs
and baking the breads,
washing the linens and sheets,
lifting water from the well
and gathering the olives from dusty,
silver-tinged branches,
picking the lemons—ripe
off the overflowing trees,
their tongues accustomed
to sun-scorched bitterness.

LEARNING CASTENET

What have they taught your hands—

the trot and gallop of your fingers

on a dust-risen path through sage

and pine and blue-bright sky—

your long mane untangling behind you,

your eyelids closed

as you pave the beat in your blood.

IT HAPPENS IN ITALY

that evening we veered
off the Piazza il Campo
(where the fountain's water
still rises from
an ancient acqueduct),

down the medieval,
cobbled alley where
we found
the atelier shop—
in the window, a gown

the Queen of Swans
must have left
behind, a promise
or a wish
for some human
to behold. My daughter,
who wears plaid shirts
and skinny jeans, who favors

no boy at 15, stared
into the glass, turned
to me: *Mom,*
I will be married in that dress.

ON VIEWING CARAVAGGIO'S THE CONVERSION OF ST. PAUL, 1601.

Santa Maria del Popolo, Rome.

At first all you notice is the hefty body
of the horse, and under its raised leg, a man
sprawled on the ground, overcome
by a vision that has wrenched away his control,
sword dropped at his side, eyes shut
and arms upraised—see how the light
holds on to his outstretched hand,
how he is left—like the viewer—
in the shock of this light, all else deep
in shadow, even the people behind you
all herded to this spot, to be struck
by this moment
that has not stopped shining.

UPON ENTERING KEATS' HOUSE

No nightingales sang,
no ancient urns
mused aloud,
    But the air
in the midst of wide quietness,
the air met me
with a weight, a texture
like vellum bearing
an onslaught of lost words
my whole body read at once.

JOHN KEATS, ON MEETING LEIGH HUNT

An era in my existence, he called it,
that October morning Keats walked
the five miles from Clerkenwell to meet him.
I imagine his quickened step, his audible
breath as the approached the Vale,
the whitewashed cottage where Hunt lived among
prints of my mythic scenes and busts of heroes.
Kindly Leigh Hunt, mover and shaker among painters
and poets and large thinkcrs of Liberal mind;
such conversational eloquence
they must have exchanged; such clasping
of appreciative hands.
Though Keats would eventually surpass him
by light-years, for now, there was this first
meeting as of two great constellations—imagine
the fierceness and reach of such light.

PIAZZA SAN MARCO,

Venice

Wind-chilled
from our vaparetto ride,
we entered that first night,
dwarfed by stone archways,
columns rooted in shadow,

hawkers darting around us—
glowing winged things spun
from their hands and into the air—
parachutes or birds?
midget angels—we could not tell;

in the distance we saw a window
lit with a thousand-tiered
chandelier like a wedding cake
made for a doge.
We might have been walking

though a trance, or the scene
before a dream takes hold.
Somewhere,
an orchestra
sifted notes through air.

EX

all that heat
and singlemindedness
that certainty and surge—

did it dissolve or disperse
explode expire
melt or meld or merge

into the invisible
molecules we inhale
the traceries

and ghosts of stars that—
light years ago—
spelled out his name.

BOOK WELL

I watched
my daughter
approach,
peer,
then fall
into the *deep-*
delved earth
Keats spoke of,
the *waters taught*
by thirst
Emily wrote,
not for
one second
did I try
to save
her.

ON SEPTEMBER 19

I think of Keats, walking the hills
beyond Winchester, as if he was
the first witness
to barred clouds and stubble fields
warmed by low-angled light.
This struck me so much in my Sunday's walk
that I composed upon it, he wrote his friend.
He passed to us the hedge crickets,
the redbreast's song, this richly
dying day we inhabit, mellow
air, and gourds brimming with ripeness
to the core, on the cusp
of breaking.

AT FOURTEEN

My daughter tells me she doesn't like
the light of late afternoon, those hours
when the sun
is drawing down and the air
takes on a molten hue
that makes her think of autumn.
I hate fall, she says, the beauty
of the leaves
doesn't make up for their dying.
I don't know how to refute her,
nor can I manage to agree, looking still
to hold those moments
of ochre-gold, before the falling
my daughter already can't help but see.

THE ROOM WHERE KEATS IS NOT

Rome

though they name him everywhere—
on the walls, shadowed
in dim light under glass;
his life mask, *a perfect*
copy of my dear brother, sister Fanny said,
except for the compression of the lips
as they must be under plaster;
the cracked 1818 *Endymion*;
and his letters, sprinkled with burnt red
sealing wax, ghostly words to his beloved:
In the hopes of entirely re-establishing my health
I shall leave England for Italy this week. . .

As near as I get to him
may be this lock of hair, snipped off
and pinned here: *the colour of brown. . .*
a yellowish look in some lights, his hair,
long, thick, exquisitely fine and running into ringlets,
Leigh Hunt said of his friend:
manly in spirit as his looks were beautiful.

And the marble fireplace
beside the narrow bed
where he died—
I press my hands
to its cool surface, the hearth
where Severn cooked *simple suppers*
of beef and a vegetable
while Keats was alive and needing to eat,
though fevered and cough-ridden,
wasting in frame with only
a posthumous existence left,
he was here   such a long ways away
and never again.

WHEN THE DOCTOR LOOKED AT THE ULTRASOUND OF MY SHOULDER AND SAID: "WELL YOU HAVE A 52-YEAR-OLD ROTATOR CUFF AFTER ALL. . . "

I thought of our dishwasher,
born 26 years before we moved in.
Just last week, it coughed up
its last spume of water. It gurgled,
then stopped, just like that. The death
rattle of silverware and dishes
that had to be removed,
laid in the porcelain sink and scrubbed
by hand, my hands that, at 52, still
oddly enjoy the splash of warm water falling
on my skin, and the way soap bubbles
sparkle under kitchen light,
such iridescent verve—I believe they would whistle
if they could—though every second
they are dying, and every second
they are born.

WHEN THE FLOOD

of blood burst the banks
in my father's brain,

the surgeon rushed in with
his sponges and his hands, his

inconceivable eye. He cleared out
the mess, and since that day the drying

air keeps whispering my father's name, the sun
keep slicing its way through cloud and mist.

EARLY SEPTEMBER, MY FATHER

Already it's the season of decrease—
afternoon light
sharper, darkness
reaching down earlier
when I walk the field with the dog
each evening. The stars appear
too soon,
too much change
catching up, the bleeding
that came to my father's brain,
the surgeon's hand like a god's hand
that stopped the leak,
the twilight
still coming down.

A LONG DEEP RUN

The doctor of rehabilitation spoke to us
of the *marathon* of my father's recovery
from traumatic brain injury,
not a sprint or a 440,
but a long deep run.
He spoke of jagged mountain peaks,
one summit achieved, then another
discovered ahead, awash
in steep sunlight and snow.
Rapt, I listened
as the doctor described
the terrible beauty and poetry
of my father's life right now.

COMA

In twilit state
may my father's
brain find rest.
May ion swords
cease their glare
and clash.
May he surrender
and the blue-
purpling sky immerse him
for a time.
May stars
burn clear—spell out
constellations of his living name.

WHEN PEOPLE ASK: HOW CAN YOU WRITE IN A BUSY CAFE

Violin concertos and conversations
criss-cross. Espresso machines churn
their steam into air—
engines of noise
      hollowing a tunnel through which I move
alone toward a pinprick of light
that may be the panes
from my grandmother's
kitchen windows; it may be the lost
flame from my grandfather's cigar.

TEENAGE DAUGHTER

I'd been warned
of tempestuous seas
with wakes of long silences,
rains of moody sleet
pockmarking the house.

Here
now, a squall
comes—but brief—
it leaves
a great shining in its place.

THE DAY IT HAPPENED

The date on the calendar
took on a glow
like the bioluminescence
that flares up in the sea at night—

it scoured our breath,
hurled us—
sunken depths—

we would swim there from now on.

MY FATHER, RECOVERING FROM BRAIN INJURY

People nod and smile,
then move on, I sense
they assume, at 85,
he's had his share of life,
what's the deal, why expect
or ask for more?
I can't explain how the hair
returning to my father's scalp
is like a sky filling with silver lightning,
that my father is large enough to contain
Whitman's multitudes—
a man of flesh and myth,
and that, in the labyrinth of my life,
he has been both the minotaur
and the one who has rescued with the thread.

FOLLOWING MY FATHER

When I arrive to visit him, recovering
from a traumatic brain bleed seven months ago,
my father is slathering his English muffin
with peanut butter, slicing into his sunnyside-up eggs
because there are no tubes left in his chest, no hole
anymore in his throat, and both his hands
can do the work they need to do.
In between bites he asks (because he can speak now)
about my daughter, my next book, be sure, he says,
to tell him when it comes out.
Later his hand grips the steel bars of the walker he uses
to move away from the bed where he lay all those months
in a space where we could not follow,
I follow him now
along the hallway of the wing he will soon
leave, the walker steering him onward—out toward
his bright and waiting life.

A GOOD MORNING

In faux-leather ballet flats
you feel the solid
press of your soles on pavement.

Already, forsythia
pour honeyed
gleam into air.

Secret birds make
a joyous ruckus
in bushes blushing green.

Yesterday (you're certain)
you wrote one darn good line.
You conquered at least

one fear; forgave (for the moment)
one bitter family member.
This morning, you wallow

in gladness—right now
your axis
tilts that much closer to luck.

PILGRIM

Call me a sucker but I'll buy
any book of poetry
if I find one line, one poem
about John Keats in its pages,
as if spotting another
traveler on the trail past near
meadows, over still streams listening
for the nightingale I've never heard.
Let me join you; join me, I might say
quietly to the poet as we embark,
plodding again toward truth or beauty
or if we're lucky some semblance of both,
as we seek some kind of balm
for that load of immortality Keats spoke of,
its awful weight on the heart.

AT KEATS' GRAVE,

Non-Catholic Cemetary, Rome.

I found the granite lyre,
the raised letters: *Here lies one*
whose name was writ in water.
Among the cypress and pine, loud birdsong,
and dark purple iris beside his stone,
a handful of withered roses lay sprawled,
a white rock etched with initials.
I rummaged in my pockets,
but found no flower or bead,
no chip of amber like the one I'd left
for my grandmother.
All I had was my new pen,
filled to the top with an ink
that wrote like early twilight.
I wedged it just below
Feb. 21, 1821, planted it—there.
Let the earth carry my message.

Caravaggio's MADONNA OF THE PILGRIMS

Church of Sant' Agostino, Rome

Glowing the claret-
hued folds of her gown
falling from pale
shoulder and hint
of breast as she holds
the fleshly wealth
of her naked baby;

above her
the slender
ring of light
that wasn't her idea,
almost
a footnote here
on this earth
her business—

this child,
this bearded man
this old woman,
wayfarers
on their knees,
their soles,
like hers,
bare
and dirt-scoured
from the journey.

SLEEP AFTER TRAVEL

descends
like the path
we took on Oia,
the sinuous wide-
spaced stones that made
a stairwell
to the caldera edge,
the taverna
that was ours
for hours,
bread sopped in oil,
octopus and olives,
tiny goblets of raki,
the Greek sun
slicing the water,
tipping our world
to dark.

HOW TO FIND KEATS

Hampstead, London

Take Hampstead High Street before dusk,
then left on Downshire Hill, one block until
St. John's Church where you'll veer to the right,
follow the narrow stone-flagged walk
to Wentworth Place, gated and locked for renovation
for much too long now, but still you must come
because it happens on this street—the living year, the year
of the great odes—the blue darkening turns fluent
with birdsong, everywhere their notes
become like cursive crisscrossing,
inscribing the air, ancestral
nightingales—they have taken up his song.

Andrea Potos is the author of five poetry collections, including *New Girl* (Anchor & Plume Press), *We Lit the Lamps Ourselves* (Salmon Poetry) and *Yaya's Cloth* (Iris Press). She has twice been the recipient of an Outstanding Achievement Award from the Wisconsin Library Association, and also received the James Hearst Poetry Prize from the *North American Review*. Her poems appear widely online and in print. She is a longtime bookseller in independent bookstores. She lives in Madison, Wisconsin with her family.